D1568192

POGO STICKS

From Start to Finish

Samuel G. Woods

Photographs by Amy Sweeney

BLACKBIRCH PRESS, INC.
WOODBRIDGE, CONNECTICUT

Special Thanks
The publisher and the author would like to thank Irwin Arginsky,
Bruce Turk and Myrna Jargowsky for their generous help in
putting this project together.

Published by Blackbirch Press, Inc.
260 Amity Road
Woodbridge, CT 06525

e-mail: staff@blackbirch.com
Web site: www.blackbirch.com

Printed in Singapore

10 9 8 7 6 5 4 3 2 1

Photo Credits: All photographs ©Amy Sweeney, except page 13: ©Culver
Pictures, and page 28: ©SBI Enterprises, Inc.

If you would like more information about SBI Enterprises, Inc., call
(800) 764-6784 or log onto the company web site www.pogosticks.com.

Library of Congress Cataloging-in-Publication Data
Woods, Samuel G.
Pogo sticks: from start to finish / by Samuel G. Woods.
      p.   cm. — (Made in the U.S.A.)
   Includes index.
   ISBN 1-56711-482-2
   1. Pogo sticks—Juvenile literature. 2. Manufacturing processes—
Juvenile literature. [1. Pogo sticks.] I. Title. II. Made in the U.S.A.
TS2301.T7   .W56 2001
688.7'2—dc21   00-011946

Contents

Ninja Turtles. Tickle Me Elmo. Furbys. Most toys that are "hot" today are not around tomorrow. Some toys, however, have lasted for generations. These "classics" tend to be the simple toys— ones that offer good, old-fashioned fun. The Slinky. Rocking horses. Pogo sticks.

Today, pogo sticks are more popular with kids than they have been in decades. Each year, hundreds of thousands of pogo sticks are purchased by children and adults around the world. How is this special toy made?

 Pogo sticks have been popular for generations.

A Jumpin' Business

The world's largest and oldest maker of pogo sticks can be found in a small town in upstate New York. Each year, SBI Enterprises Inc. ships more than 300,000 pogo sticks to its customers. Operating from their factory in Ellenville, New York, the company assembles, packages, and ships their products to customers in nearly every corner of the globe.

 Nearly finished pogos are pushed to the packing area. **Inset:** *Rows of pogo tips.*

Pieces of Pogo

Most pogos are built with 20 to 35 pieces. Many of the parts are made from steel. Because pogos need to take so much bouncing, hopping, pounding, and jumping, they cannot be made from plastic or other light materials.

 A worker uses a large machine to bend metal pieces for the steps.

The first pieces to be created are the steps. Each step is made by bending and then attaching two steel plates. Before they are shaped, the steel plates are called blanks.

Two machines are needed to create steps. First, a press is used to bend each steel plate up at a 90° angle. After the plate is put in place, the 2 ends of the press come together with a force equal to 35 tons of pressure. When the press opens, one half of a step is done.

Left: *Flat blanks are bent into the pieces below. Two of these pieces will make a set of steps.*

7

Step by Step

The bent step halves are moved to another area of the factory. There, one half is joined to another. The pieces are secured by steel rivets, which are like bolts. When the two pieces are joined, a step is created.

 A powerful machine drives a rivet through the steel step pieces.

🌀 The riveting machine drives a steel pin into both step pieces.
Inset: *Two step pieces are riveted together.*

Inside Tips

In another area of the factory, pogo bottoms and tips are assembled. The pogo stick's bottom section is made by placing a rubber tip over the end of a steel tube. The tube has a slot cut into it. This will allow the pogo's spring action to move easily up and down.

Left and below: A small metal disc reinforces the rubber-tipped bottom.

Slots in the pogo tube allow the spring action to move up and down.

The rubber tip is hammered on for a secure fit.

The tip is made of a material called Nitrile. It looks like plain rubber, but it is a very high-tech, extra-strong mix of rubber and other materials.

Before the tip is placed on the tube, a steel disc is placed inside. This prevents the tube from cutting into the tip as the pogo bounces.

11

A Hoppin' History

Pogo sticks are something of an Ellenville, New York, tradition. In fact, pogos have been coming out of Ellenville for more than 80 years.

Modern pogo making began with a man named George Hansburg. He was a toy designer from Illinois who wanted to create a jumping stick that would be fun for kids as well as adults. Hansburg said his idea came from a jumping stick he had seen and heard about in Germany.

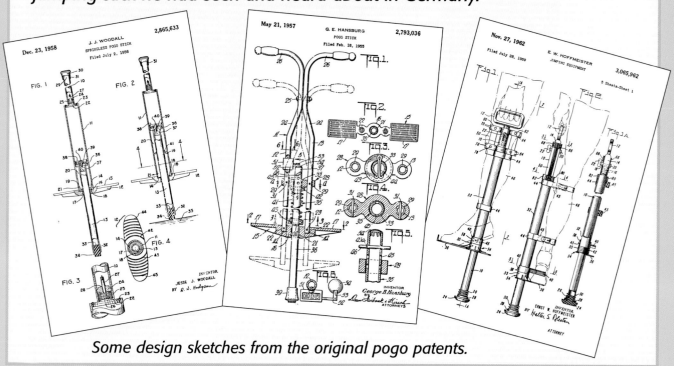

Some design sketches from the original pogo patents.

Pogo legend has it that the very first pogo was created in the Asian country of Burma (now called Myanmar). The first pogo was supposedly made by a poor farmer who could not afford shoes for his daughter, named Pogo. By attaching a small stick to a large pole, the farmer fashioned a "jumping stick." This allowed his daughter to travel over all types of land without shoes. A German visitor to Burma saw the jumping stick and created a similar contraption upon his return to Germany. From there, came George Hansburg's inspiration. By 1919, wooden pogo sticks were being sold commercially in Germany, mostly through Gimbel Brothers department stores.

Hansburg set up a factory in an area near Ellenville and began producing wooden pogo sticks. In only a short time, a "pogo craze" took over the American Northeast.

Women with pogo sticks in 1922.

Throughout the "Roaring '20s" thousands of "flapper girls" and dashing, carefree men could be found hopping and bouncing nearly everywhere on pogos. Even the famous Ziegfeld Follies (dancing girls) performed on pogo sticks for a while! Public stunts and jumping marathons were also a popular form of entertainment.

In 1947, George Hansburg designed the first metal pogo stick and patented it. He also re-tooled his factory so it could begin producing the new product, which he called the "Master Pogo." The Master has been made the very same way ever since.

By 1967, Hansburg was more than 80 years old. The time was right for him to sell his company and pass the pogo tradition on to someone else. That someone was Irwin Arginsky. With two other partners, Arginsky bought SBI Enterprises and launched into the pogo stick business.

Vintage wooden pogo from the 1920s.

1960s pogo

Irwin Arginsky stands in front of his "pogo museum" wall, which spans more than 80 years.

When Arginsky first bought the company, it was producing about 20,000 pogos a year. Since that time, sales have exploded. In 2000, SBI shipped more than 360,000 pogos to their customers worldwide. Arginsky says that the pogo's popularity is due to the fact that it is "a forever toy."

"There's always a need for a basic toy that will provide a challenge to a child," Arginsky says. He also believes that, in today's high-tech, computer-crazy world, parents are eager to give their kids an active, physical toy that gets them outside and provides good exercise. "It's a wonderful departure from sitting with a mouse in front of a computer screen," says Arginsky.

Greased Lightnin'

SBI's bestselling model for younger kids is called the Maverick Pogo. The middle tube of the Maverick contains a heavy steel spring. Before the spring can be placed inside the tube it must be greased. The grease reduces friction (rubbing) as the pogo moves up and down. It also allows for a smooth and quiet bouncing action.

Once the middle spring tube is complete, the pogo is ready for final assembly.

With all the sections in one area, the final assembly of the pogo can take place. First, the handle is created. To do this, a steel rod is inserted through a hole at the top of the middle tube. The fit is very tight, so the rod must be banged into position.

 Opposite: Heavy steel springs are greased before they are assembled on the pogo. *Right:* A handle is inserted at the pogo's top.

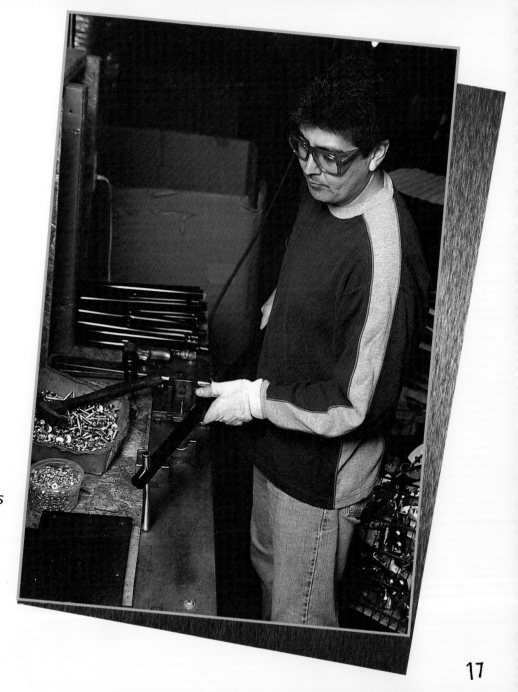

Hopping to It

Now the step is placed over the middle tube. Then the slotted tube with the tip is fitted to the middle. The unfinished assembly is placed in a special clamp that holds it on the worktable. Once in place, a heavy lever pushes the assembly together and compresses the spring inside the middle tube.

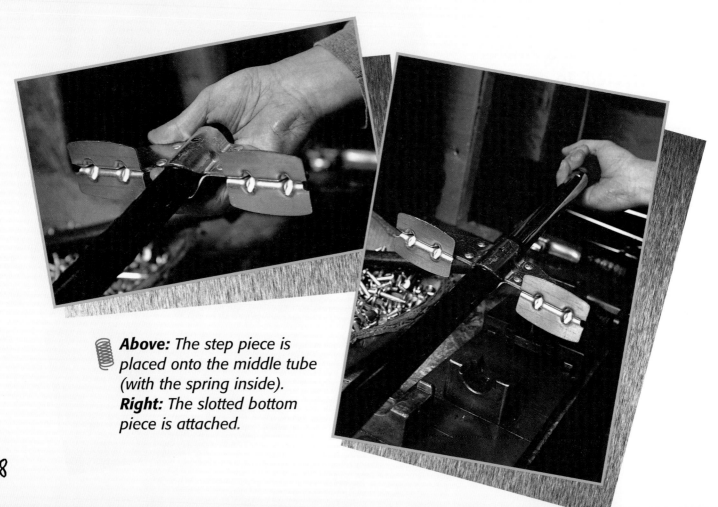

Above: The step piece is placed onto the middle tube (with the spring inside).
Right: The slotted bottom piece is attached.

A heavy lever pushes the assembly together, compressing the tube inside.

19

A steel saddle bolt holds the tube to the step. **Inset:** Nearly finished Mavericks, ready for packing.

Springtime

While the spring is being pressed, a steel saddle bolt is placed through the assembly. The saddle bolt is held in place by a steel lock nut.

When the lever is released, the spring is held tight by the saddle bolt.

The pogo is now ready for its finishing touches.

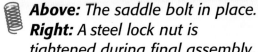

Above: *The saddle bolt in place.*
Right: *A steel lock nut is tightened during final assembly.*

JUMP to CONCLUSIONS

In 1996, SBI sold its 3 millionth pogo to one of its oldest customers: Toys "R" Us. Charles Lazarus—founder of Toys "R" Us—noted that, when he opened the doors to his very first store, pogo sticks were on his shelves. He's been selling them continuously for 52 years ever since!

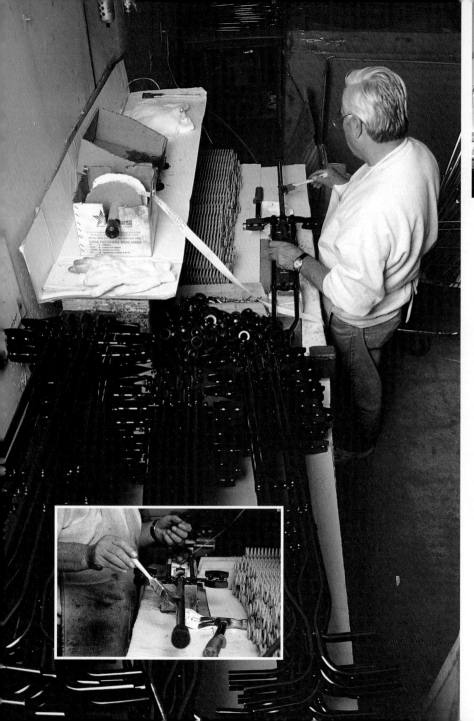

The Master

SBI's best-selling model for older kids and adults is the Master Pogo. The Master is a bit different from the one used by younger kids. The middle section is made up of two bent steel tubes (instead of one straight one). In the middle—on the outside—is a large, heavy-duty green spring.

Inset: *Greasing the bottom tube before final assembly.*
Left and top: *Compressing the Master spring on the worktable.*

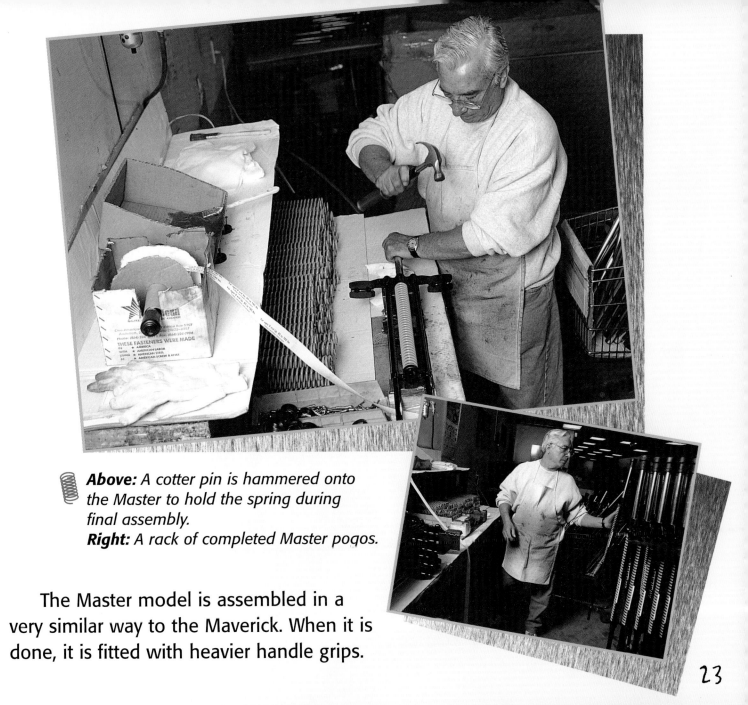

Above: A cotter pin is hammered onto the Master to hold the spring during final assembly.
Right: A rack of completed Master poqos.

The Master model is assembled in a very similar way to the Maverick. When it is done, it is fitted with heavier handle grips.

Steps and Handles

The steps and handles for each pogo are not actually attached at the factory. Instead, a plastic bag that contains these parts is included in the box. This way, the steps and handles are not damaged during shipping.

Before the first use, the steps and handles attach easily to the body of the pogo.

Brightly colored steps and handles are packed in bags and shipped in the carton.

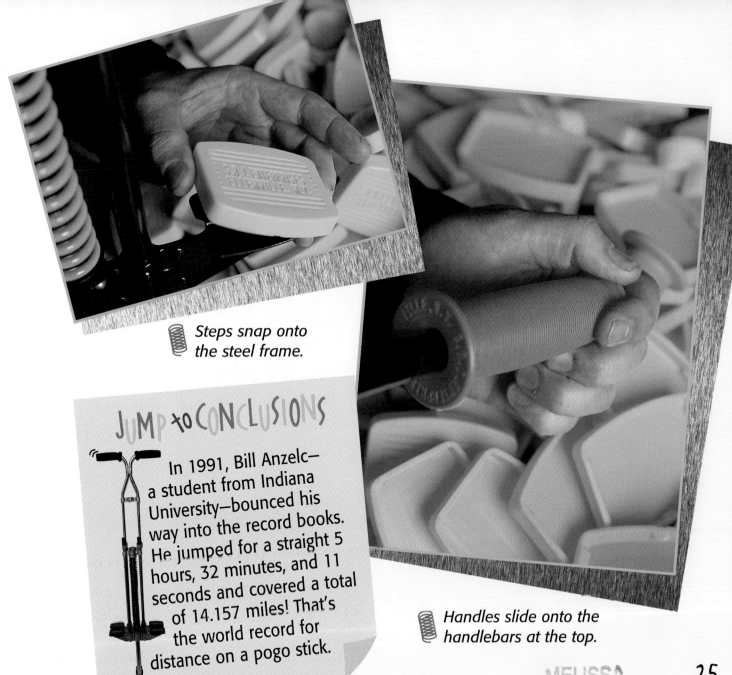

Steps snap onto the steel frame.

Handles slide onto the handlebars at the top.

JUMP to CONCLUSIONS

In 1991, Bill Anzelc—a student from Indiana University—bounced his way into the record books. He jumped for a straight 5 hours, 32 minutes, and 11 seconds and covered a total of 14.157 miles! That's the world record for distance on a pogo stick.

Packin' a Bounce

In the cartoning area, assembled pogos are placed in a long box, along with a bag of parts. An important sheet of instructions and safety rules is also included. It is very important for all users to read and follow the safety directions from the manufacturer.

 Assembled pogos are placed in their shipping cartons, along with a bag of parts.

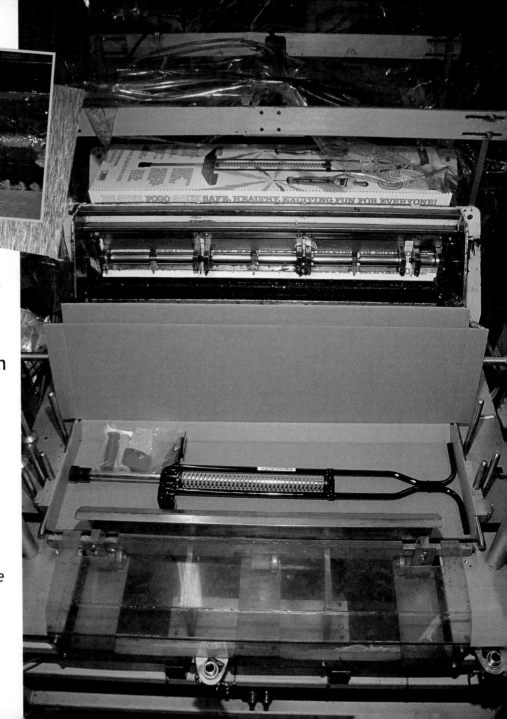

The boxes are fed through a packing machine that applies hot glue to each carton's edge. The glue is heated to more than 350° F. Once it is applied, the glue cools quickly and holds the carton closed. The packing machine can seal 2,500 pogo boxes in one 8-hour shift!

Above: *A hot glue machine coats the shipping carton for sealing.*
Right: *A cartoning machine folds and seals the box before shipping.*

Jumping for the World's Record

In 1997, a 23-year-old medical student named Gary Stewart made pure pogo history. Stewart logged a new world record when he completed 177,737 consecutive hops! The feat took him a total of 20 hours and 20 minutes.

Stewart had actually set the previous world record five years earlier (130,077 hops). He wanted to try again because The Guinness Book of World Records *spelled his name wrong while listing the first record.*

"That's why I started doing it," Stewart says, *"to get my name in that book. It was a kind of childhood dream."*

Gary Stewart, as he jumped into the record books.

Stewart's love affair with pogo sticks began in 1974, when a neighbor gave him a pogo that her daughter didn't want. "That day, my brother did 31 jumps and I stayed in the garage until I could do more than 31," Stewart recalls. Soon, he became a pogo master, doing stunts and jumping more than 4 feet in the air!

When it came time to break the Guinness record, Stewart was sponsored by Burger King for a promotion. He was given a number of custom-made double pogos that were able to do 240 jumps per minute. The hops were counted on a special pressure-sensitive steel platform. The platform counted every jump as the pogo landed.

Stewart could have gone longer, but he decided to stop when he reached 177, 737 jumps (that had special meaning to him). When he was done, Burger King promised that they would make sure Gary Stewart's name was spelled properly in the Guinness Book of World Records. And it was.

Double-springed pogo used by Gary Stewart.

Loads of Pogos

Six pogo boxes fit into each carton. When a pile of cartons is ready to be stacked, it is moved with a forklift to the loading area. There, they are labeled for delivery all over the world.

During their busy seasons, SBI loads 53-foot tractor-trailers with nearly 5,000 pogos at a time!

When they reach their final destinations, the pogos provide endless hours of challenge, exercise, and just plain fun!

 Left: *Thousands of pogos await loading and shipment.*
Right: *Pogos are fun and challenging for everyone.*

Glossary

clamp a tool used to hold things firmly in place

contraption a strange device or machine

fashioned to make or shape something

patent a legal document that gives the inventor of something the only rights to manufacture or sell the item

plate a flat piece of metal

rivet a strong metal bolt that is used to fasten pieces of metal together

For More Information

Books

Steele, Philip. *Toys and Games* (Everyday History). Danbury, CT: Franklin Watts, Inc., 2000.

Wulffson, Don L. *Toys!: Amazing Stories Behind Some Great Inventions.* New York, NY: Henry Holt and Company, Inc., 2000.

Web Site

SBI Enterprises Inc.
Learn interesting pogo facts, as well as how to care for and use a pogo stick.
www.pogosticks.com.

Index